DEAD BABIES

A SERIES OF SHORT LIFE STORIES

SANDY WAS KILLED IN A TRAGIC FIRE

BETH WAS POISONED WITH A PACIFIER

TRACEY GOT INTO MOM'S PSYCHEDELIC DRUGS

GUNTHER DIED OF SEPSIS. THANKS TO BED BUGS

JACKSON WAS LEFT TO DIE IN AN ALLEY

A TORNADO IS WHAT KILLED BABY SALLY

SEAN WAS KILLED IN A MASSIVE CAR CRASH

TONY DIED OF MEASLES. THEY THOUGHT IT WAS A RASH.

SONIA FELL ASLEEP ON THE TRACKS

A NUCLEAR EXPLOSION IS WHAT KILLED MAX

JENNY TOOK TOO MANY OF DAD'S SLEEPING PILLS

SAMMY WAS SOLD FOR HIS ORGANS. TO COVER DAD'S BILLS

FIONA WAS LEFT TO DIE IN AN ABANDONED HOUSE

FALLING INTO THE POOL. THAT'S WHAT KILLED KLAUSE

If you want to reach me.

TW: @bradgosse
IG: @bradgosse
FB: @bradgosse
TIKTOK: @bradgosse
Youtube: Search for Brad Gosse

If you want clipart from this book.
@vectortoons
VectorToons.com

THE END. WRITTEN BY BRAD GOSSE

FURIOUS GEORGE
NEEDS A SMOKE TO CALM THE FUCK DOWN

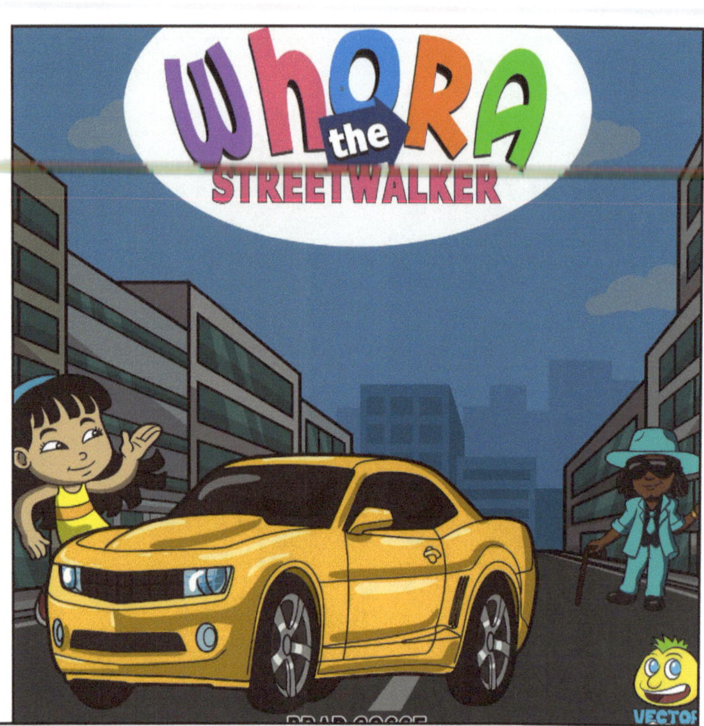

WHORA
the
STREETWALKER

CHECK OUT MY OTHER BOOKS AVAILABLE SOON

DADS SECRET FAMILY
MEET YOUR NEW HALF SIBLINGS AND SISTER MOM
BRAD GOSSE

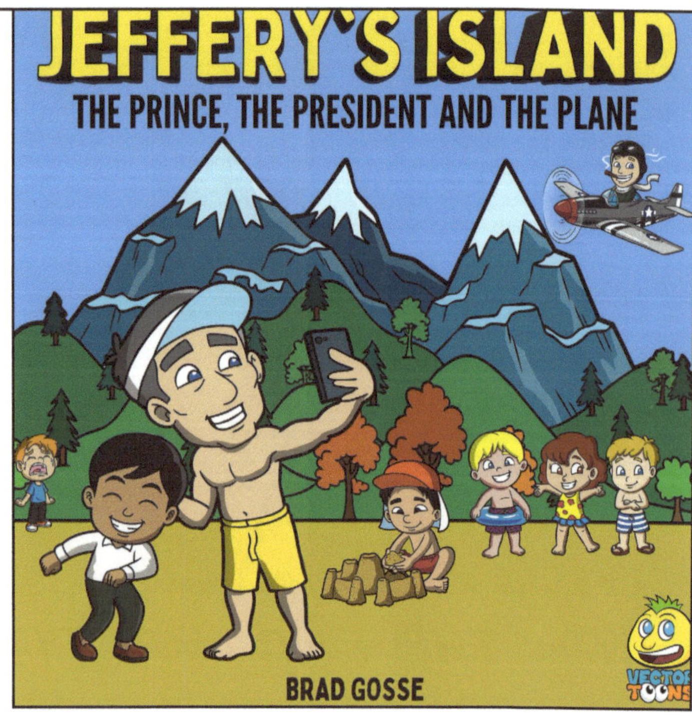

JEFFERY'S ISLAND
THE PRINCE, THE PRESIDENT AND THE PLANE
BRAD GOSSE

SCOUTS HONOR
BREAKING YOUR PROMISE TO SCOUT LEADER DAN
VECTOR TOONS

I'M NOT YOUR FATHER
KIDS GUIDE TO PATERNITY LAW
VECTOR TOONS

CHECK OUT MY OTHER BOOKS AVAILABLE SOON

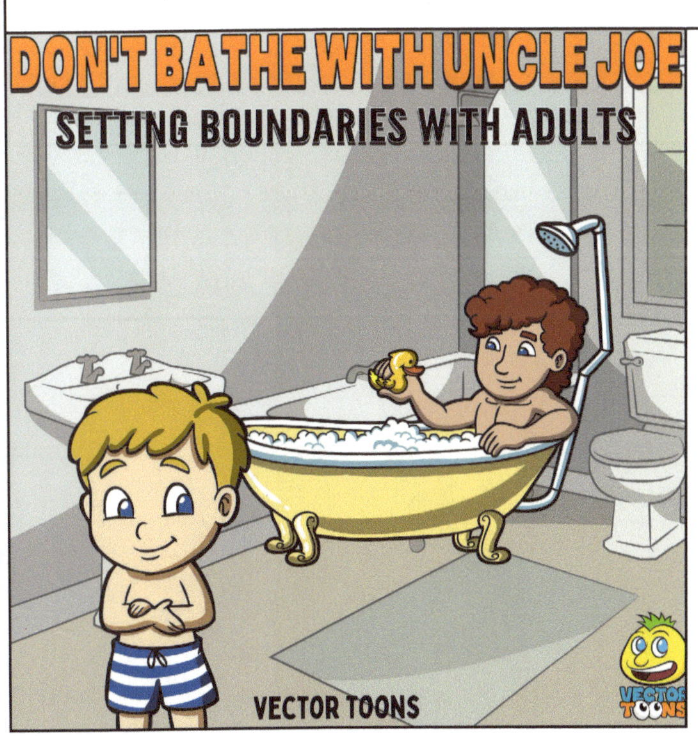

DON'T BATHE WITH UNCLE JOE
SETTING BOUNDARIES WITH ADULTS
VECTOR TOONS

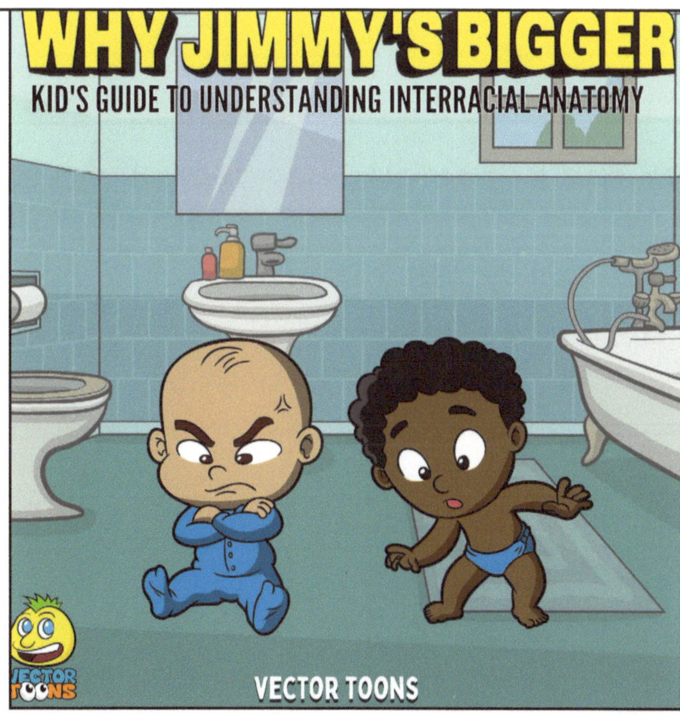

WHY JIMMY'S BIGGER
KID'S GUIDE TO UNDERSTANDING INTERRACIAL ANATOMY
VECTOR TOONS

RICH KIDS
9 REASONS THEY'RE BETTER THAN YOU
VECTOR TOONS

MY RACIST GRAN
SAYS WE STILL CAN'T TRUST THE JAPS
VECTOR TOONS

CHECK OUT MY OTHER BOOKS AVAILABLE SOON

CREEPY GUY AT THE POOL
HOW TO DEAL WITH STRANGERS WHO WATCH YOU SWIM
VECTOR TOONS

SNITCHES GET STITCHES
WHY MOM SHOULD HAVE KEPT HER MOUTH SHUT
VECTOR TOONS

DON`T TALK
UNLESS YOU WANT TO GET DAD INTO TROUBLE
BRAD GOSSE

WHEN MOM DRUNK DIALS
HOW TO BEHAVE WHEN STRANGERS COME OVER
VECTOR TOONS

CHECK OUT MY OTHER BOOKS AVAILABLE SOON

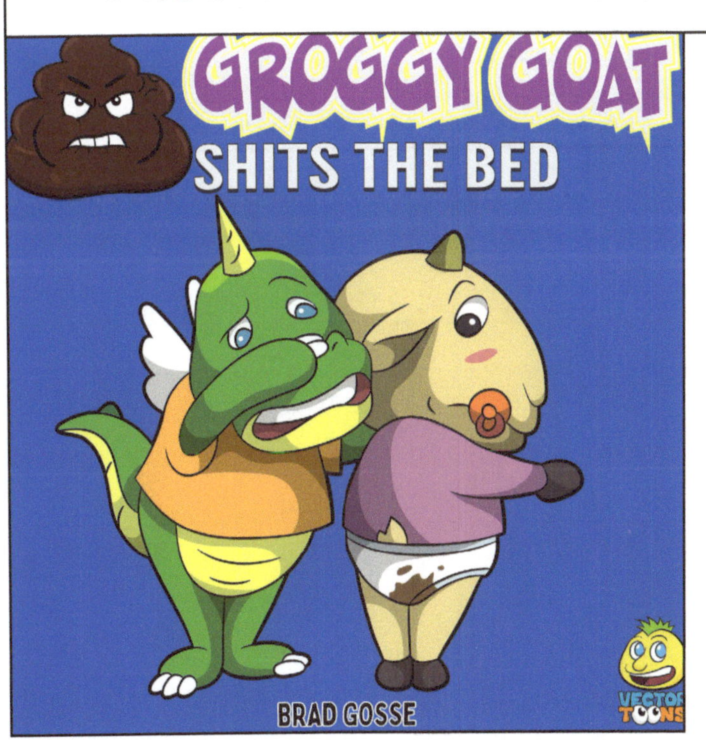

GROGGY GOAT
SHITS THE BED
BRAD GOSSE

MOUTH HERPES
AND 7 OTHER SIDE EFFECTS OF FAMILY CHRISTMAS SLEEPOVERS
BRAD GOSSE
VECTOR TOONS

BAA BAA BLACK SHEEP
DEALS WITH ANOTHER "ROUTINE" STOP

MOM MAKES ME LIE
CONFESSIONS OF AN OVERUSED PINOCCHIO

CHECK OUT MY STICKERS, CARDS AND SHIRTS
BRADGOSSE-REDBUBBLE.COM

I WANT TO
GROW OLD WITH YOU

BI-CURIOUS GEORGE
DISCOVERS SAME SEX PORNOGRAPHY